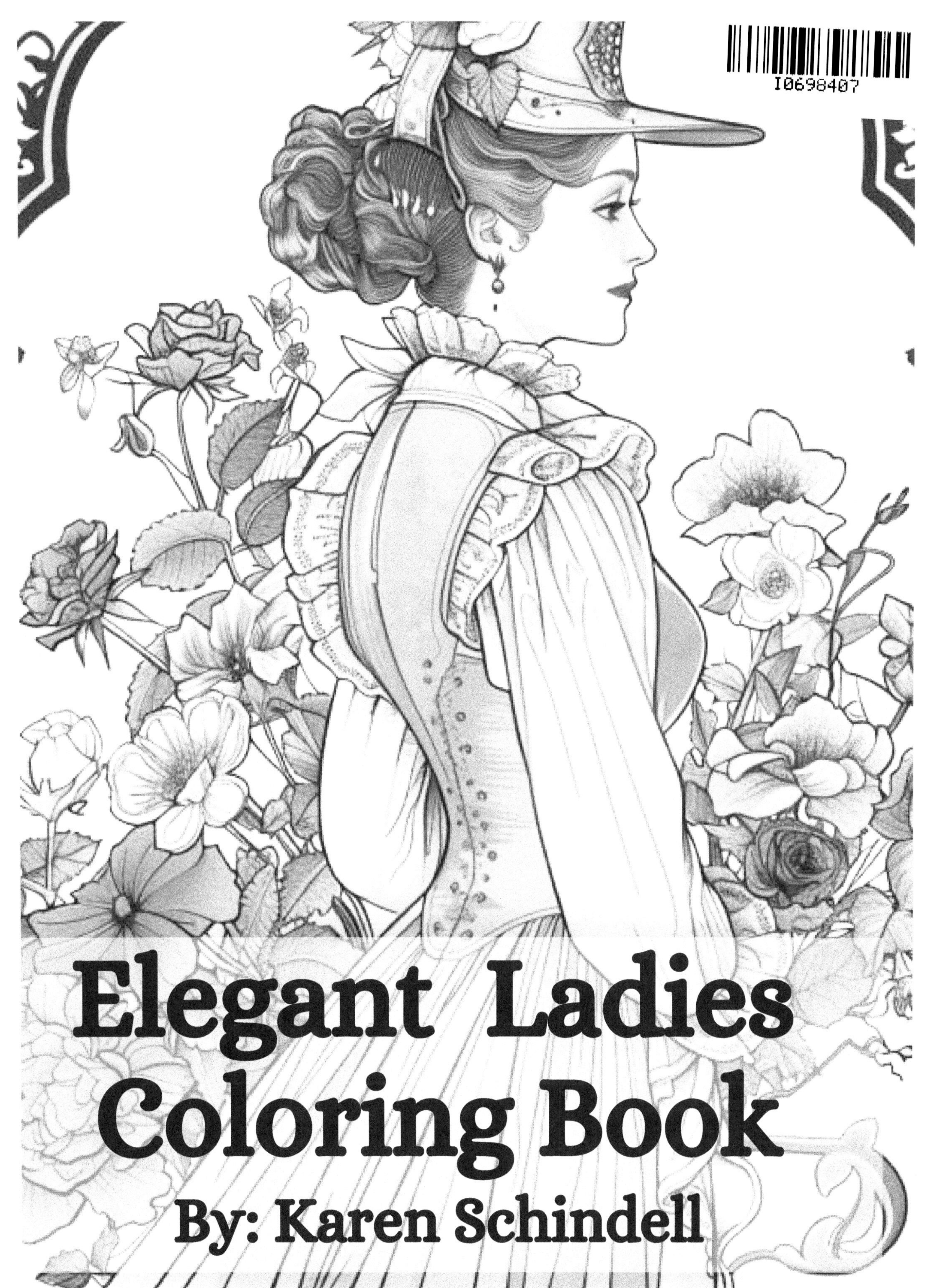

Elegant Ladies Coloring Book

By: Karen Schindell

Copywritten 2024
by: Karen Schindell

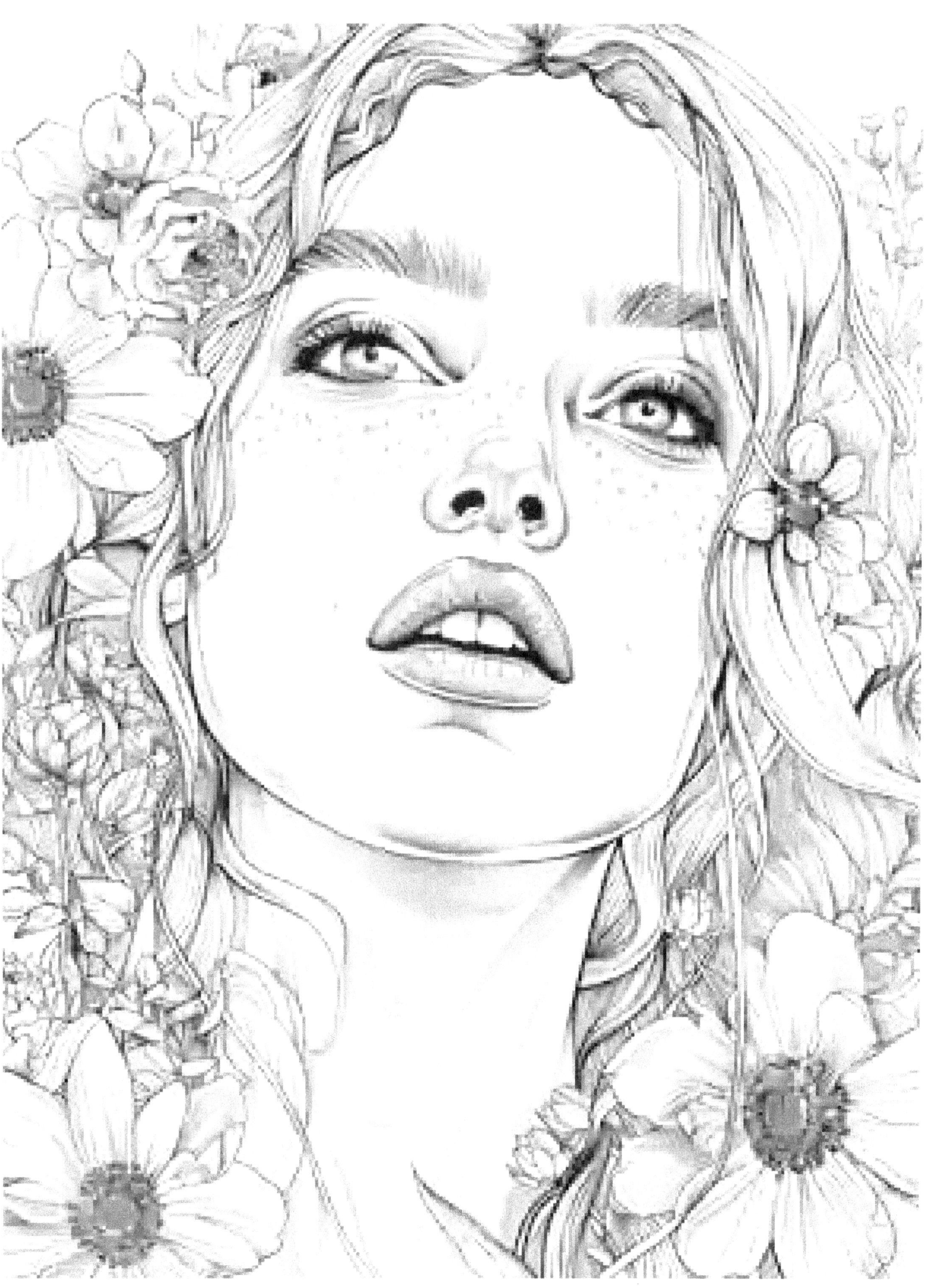

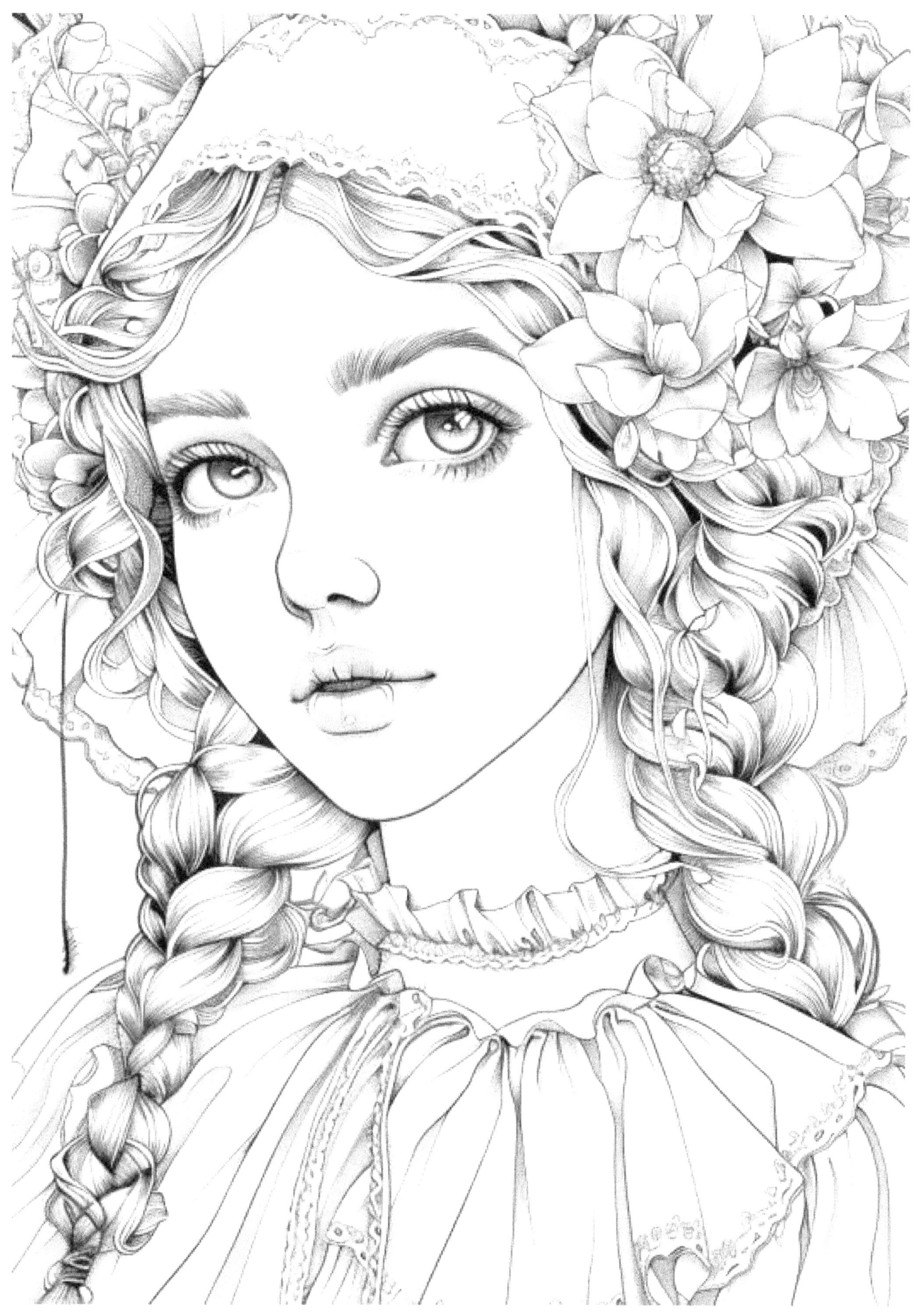

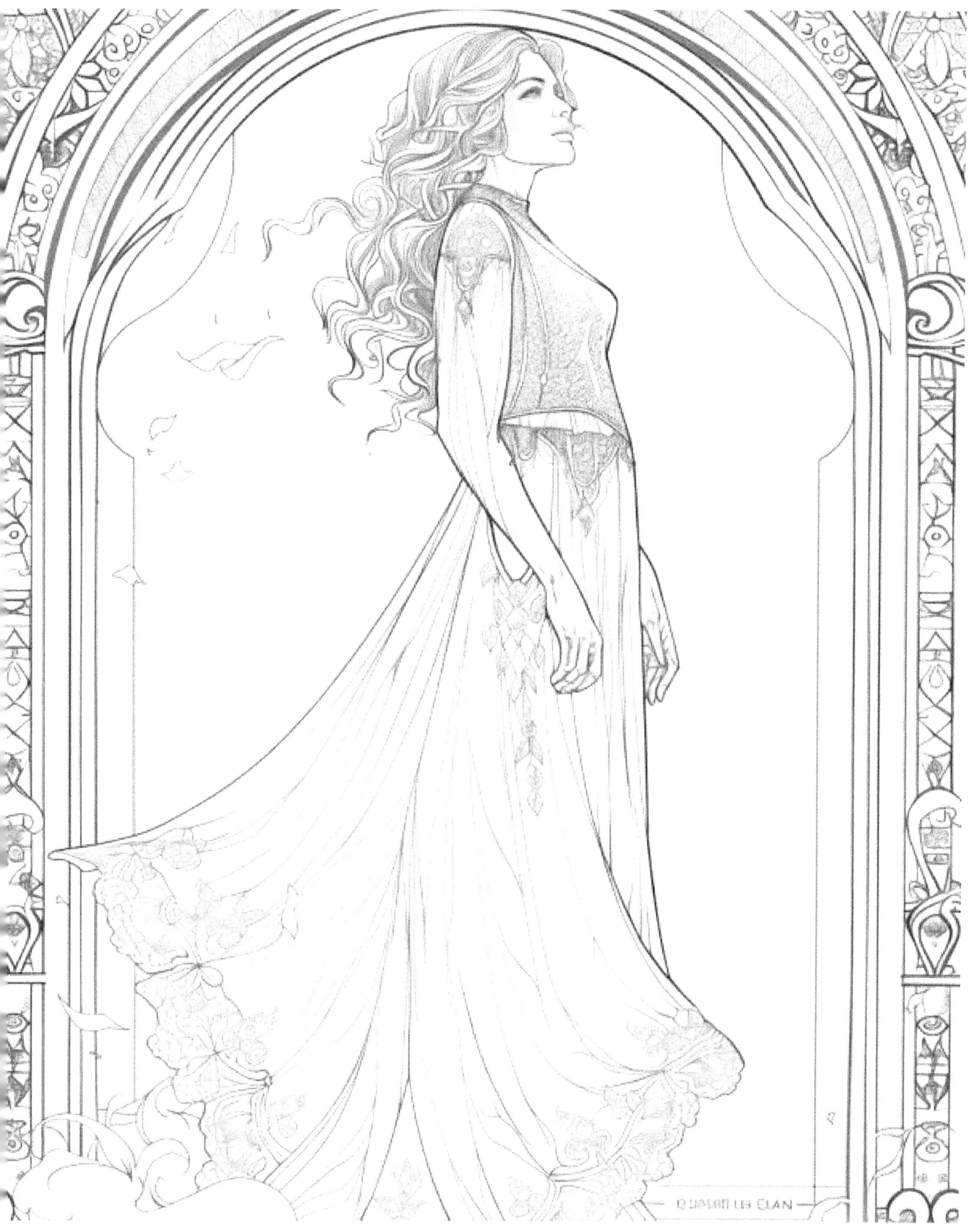

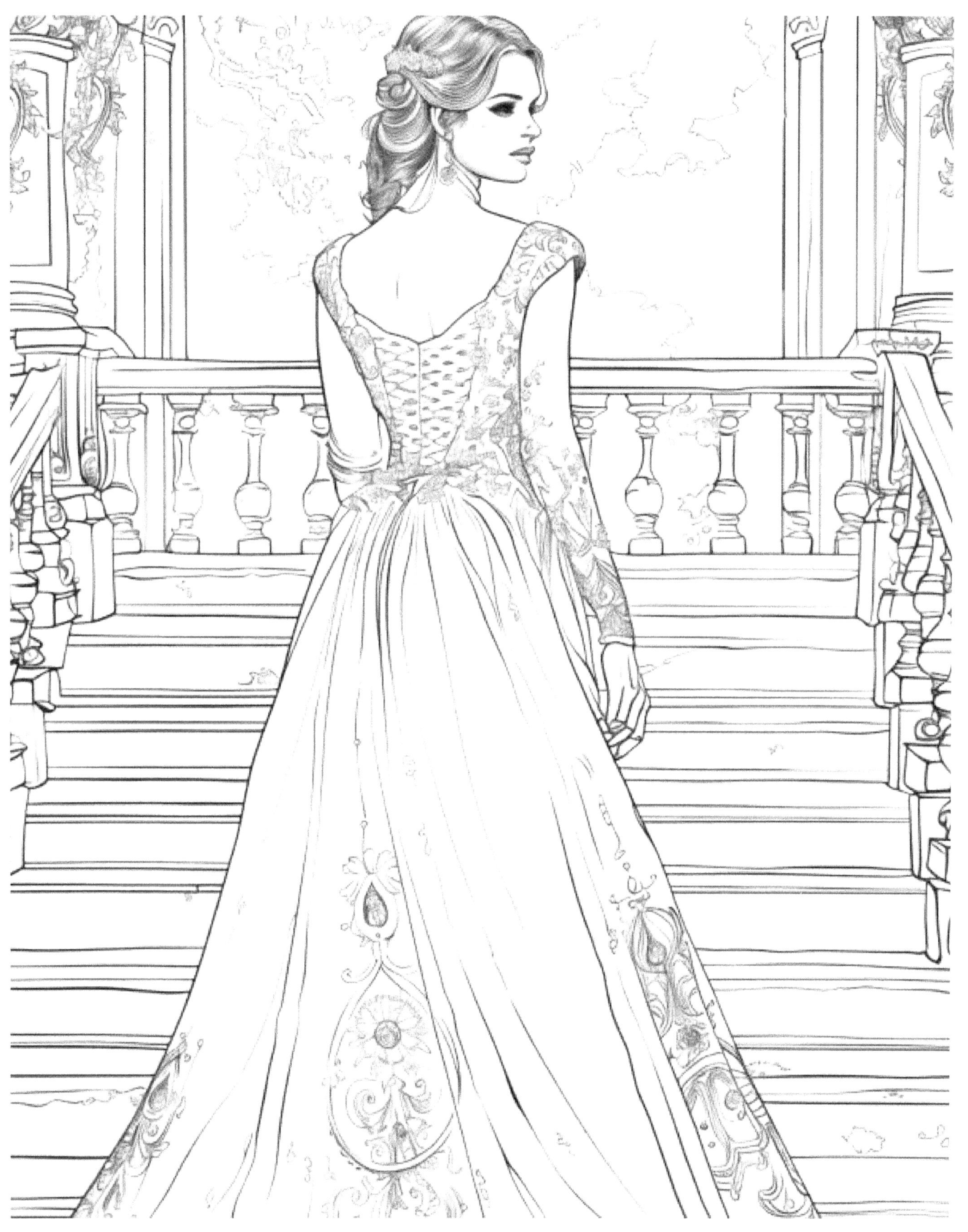

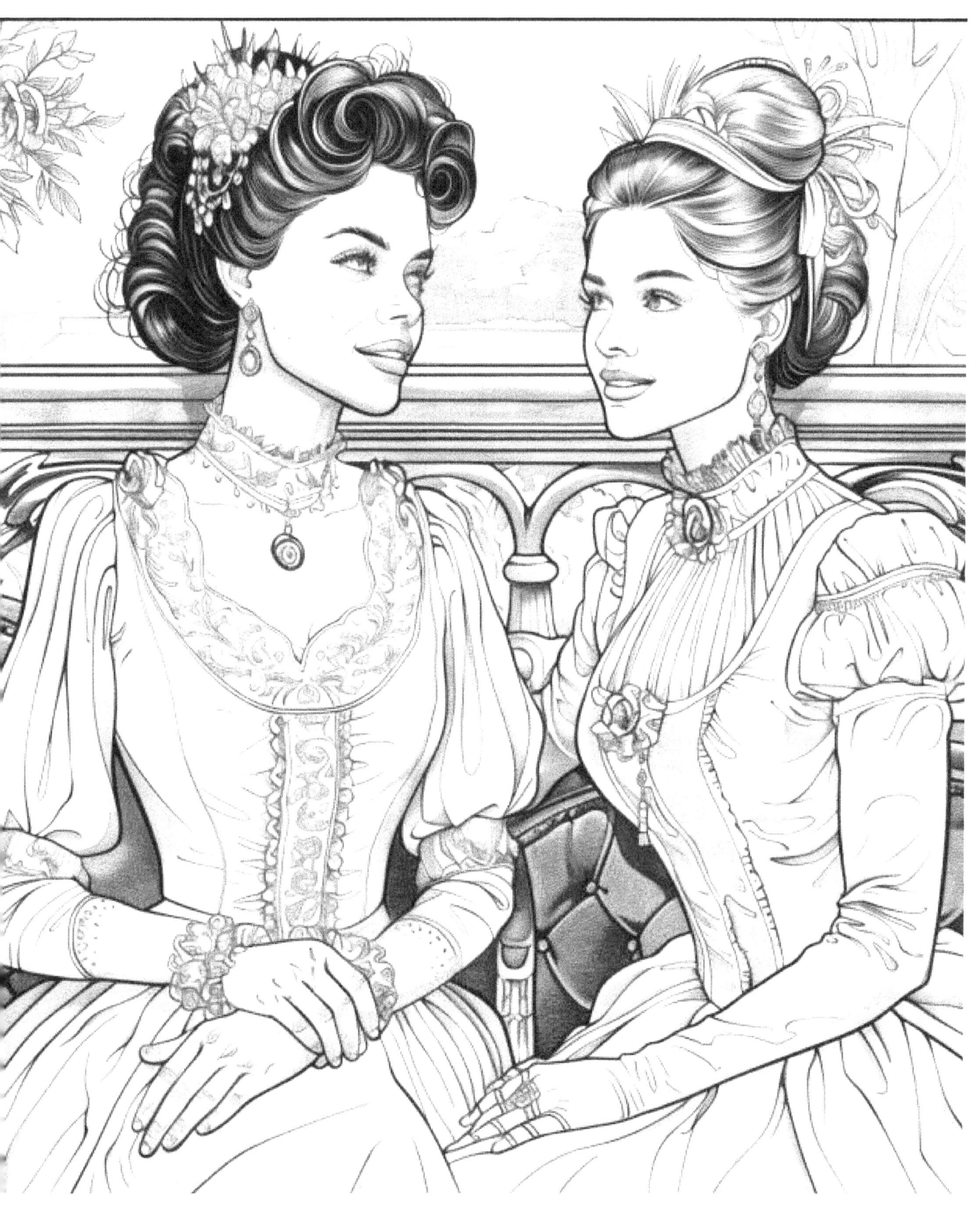

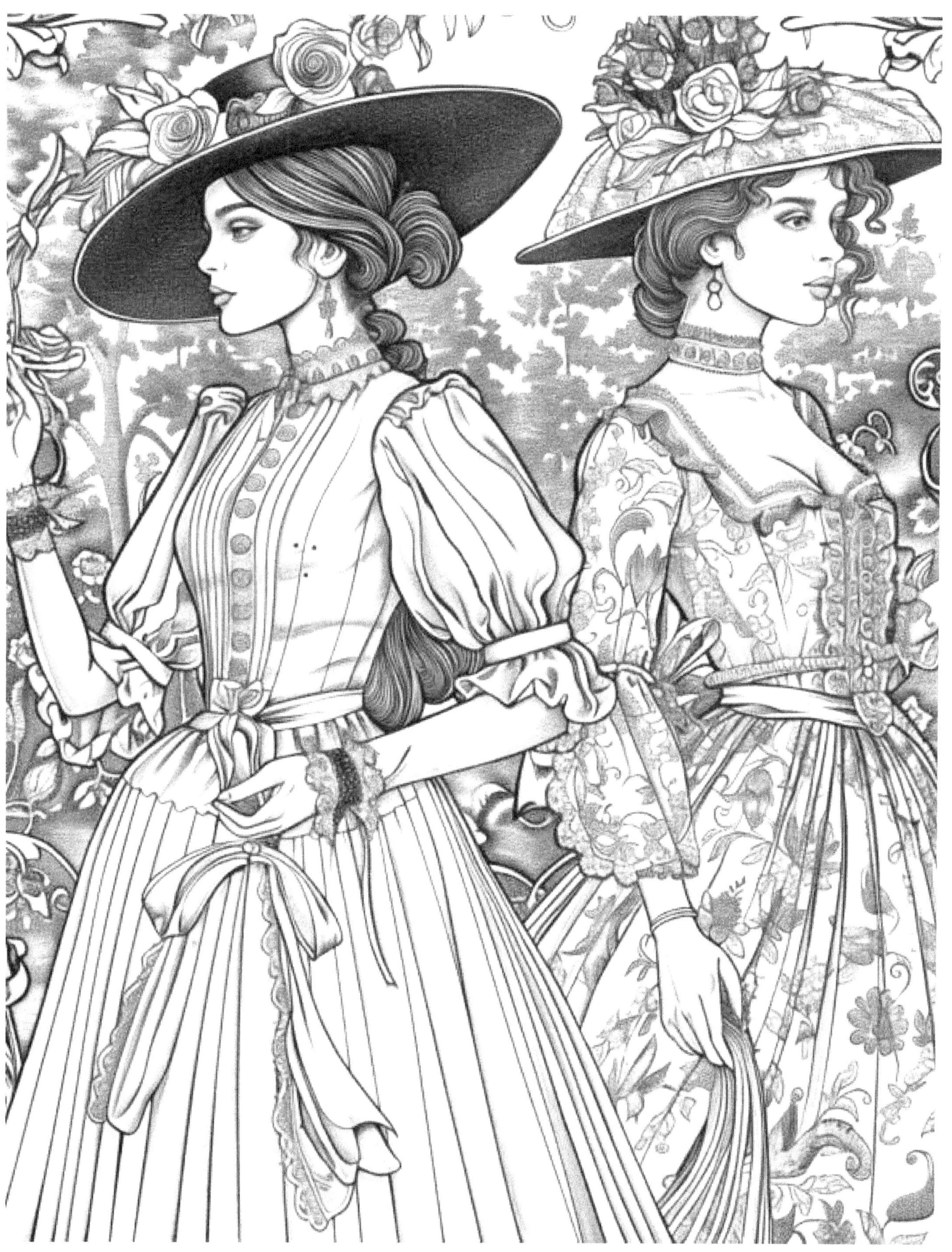

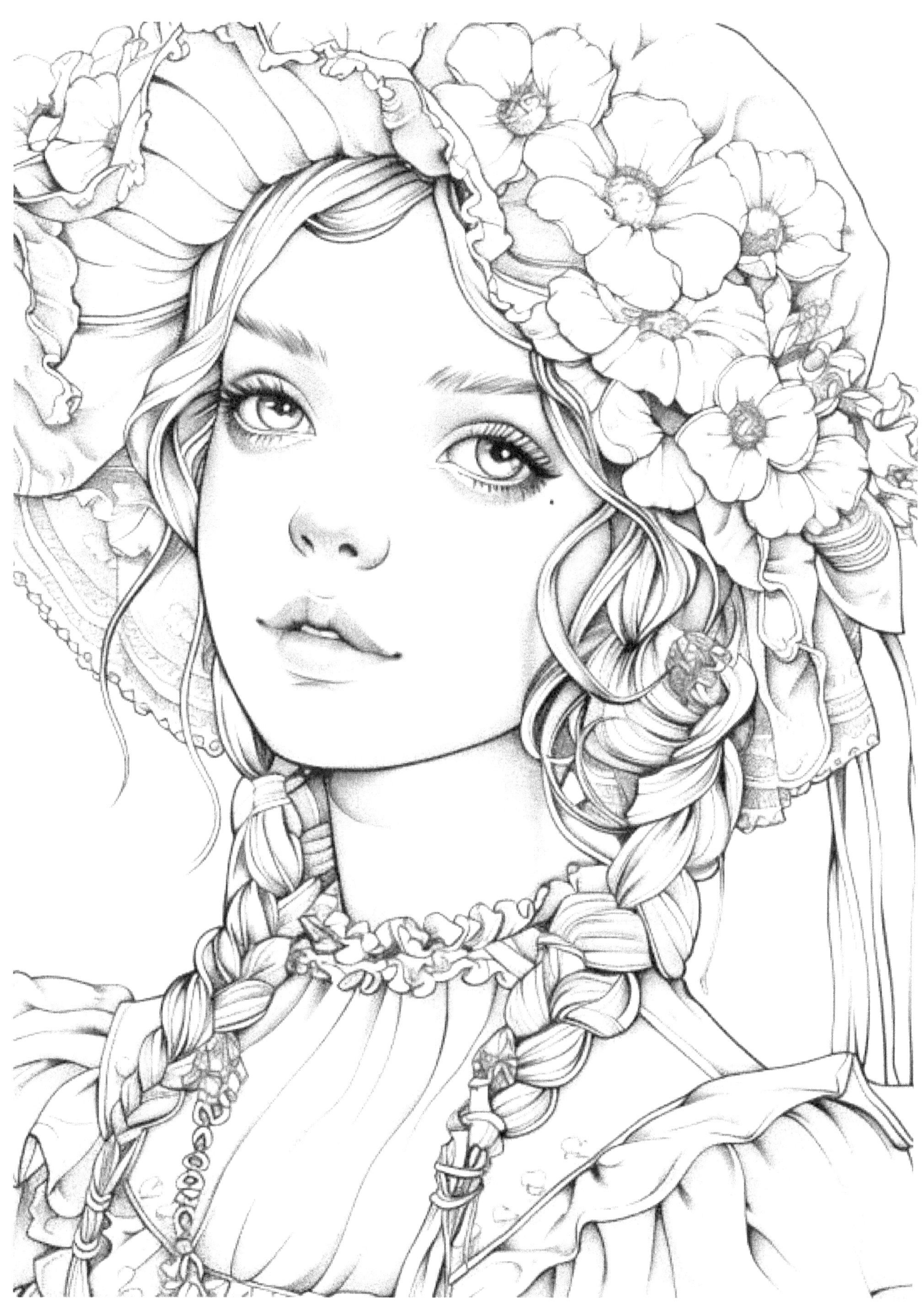

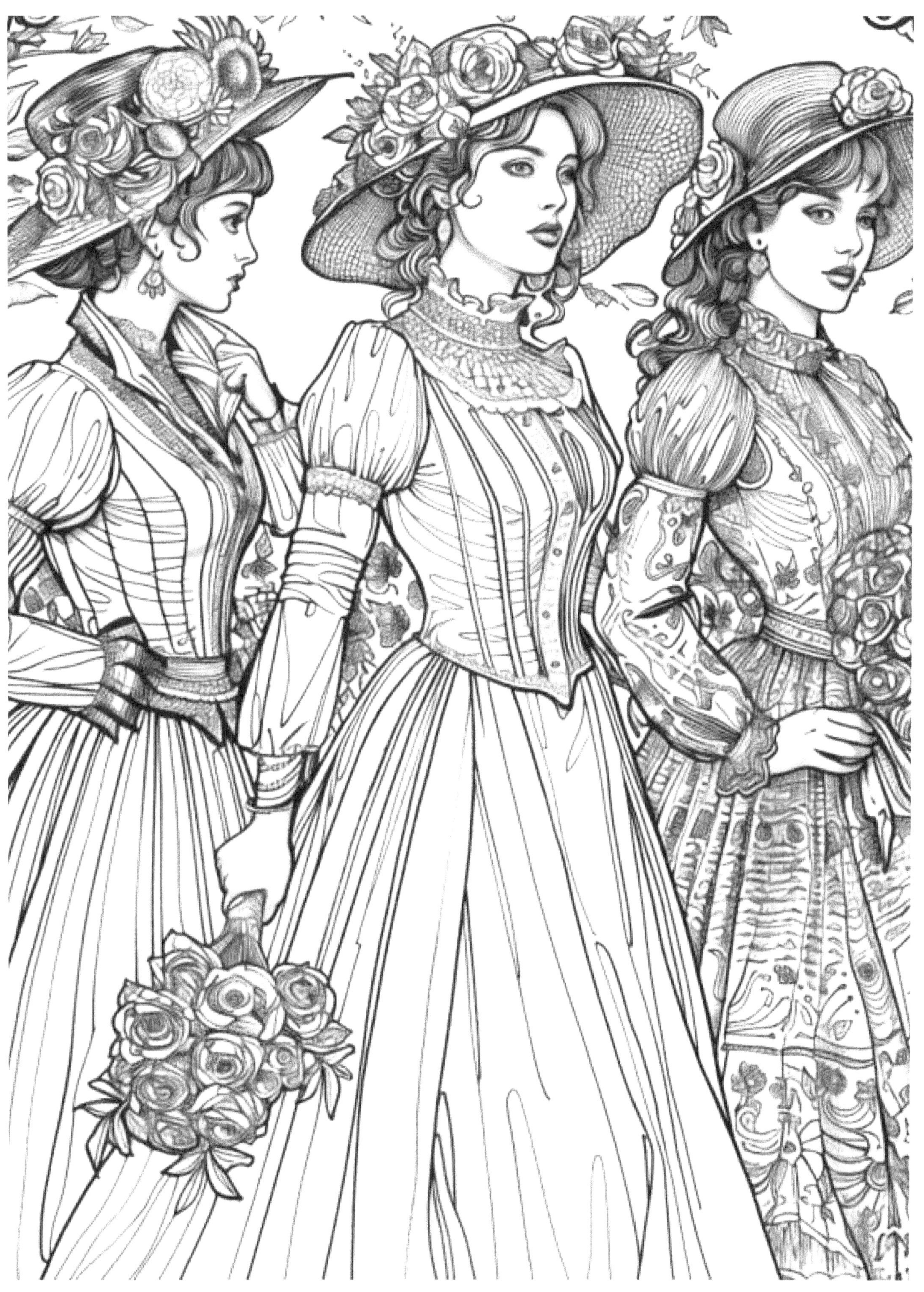

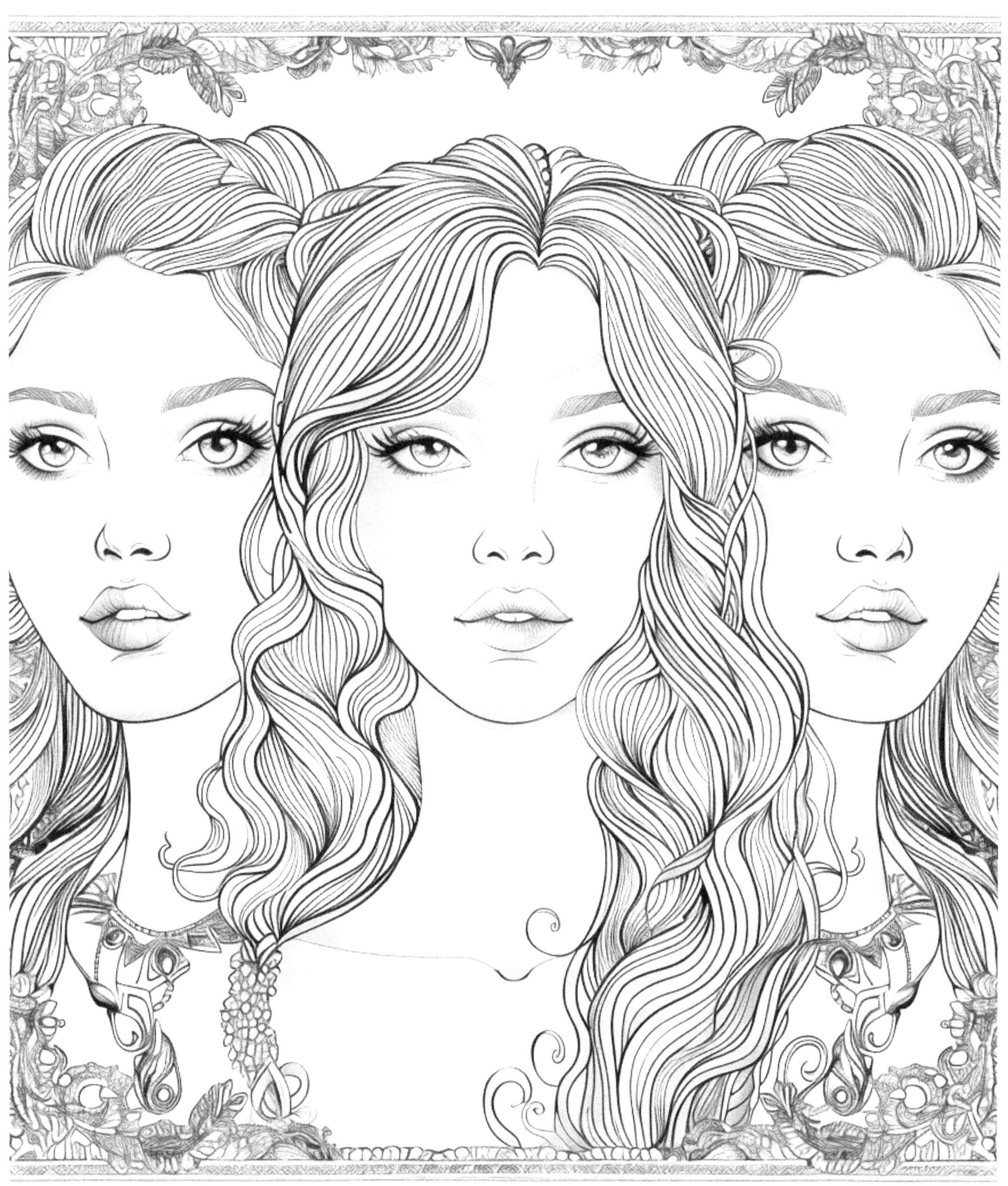

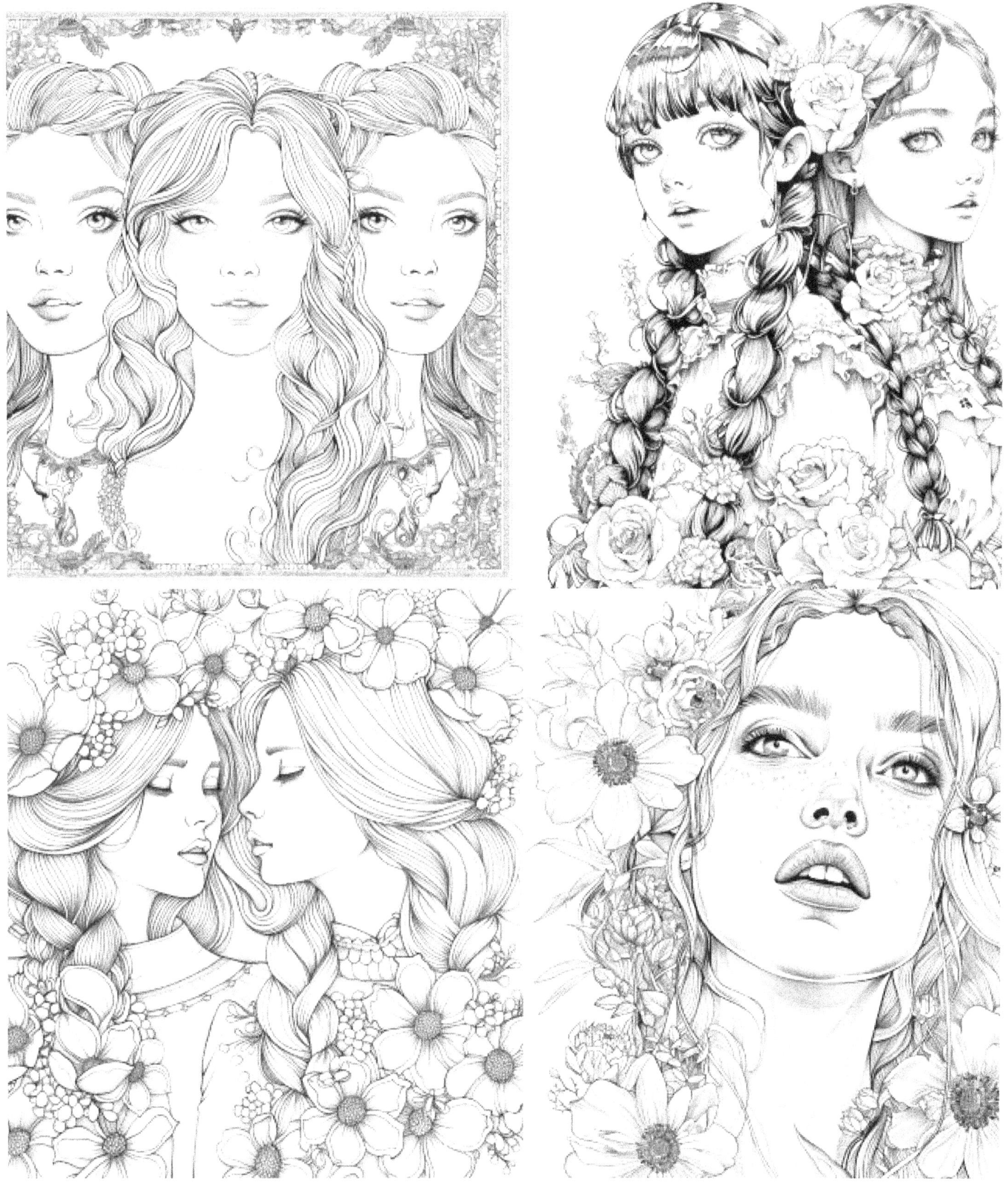

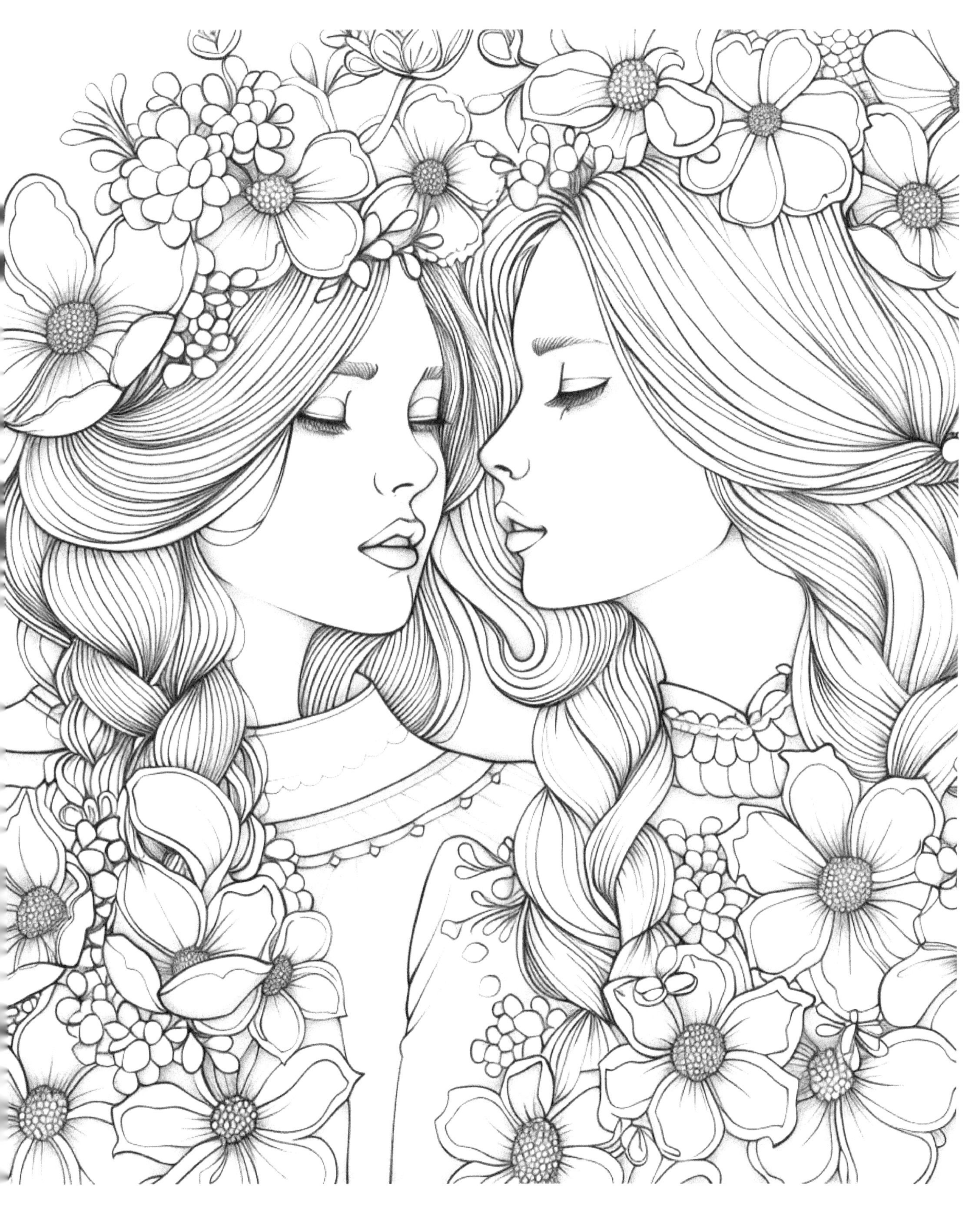

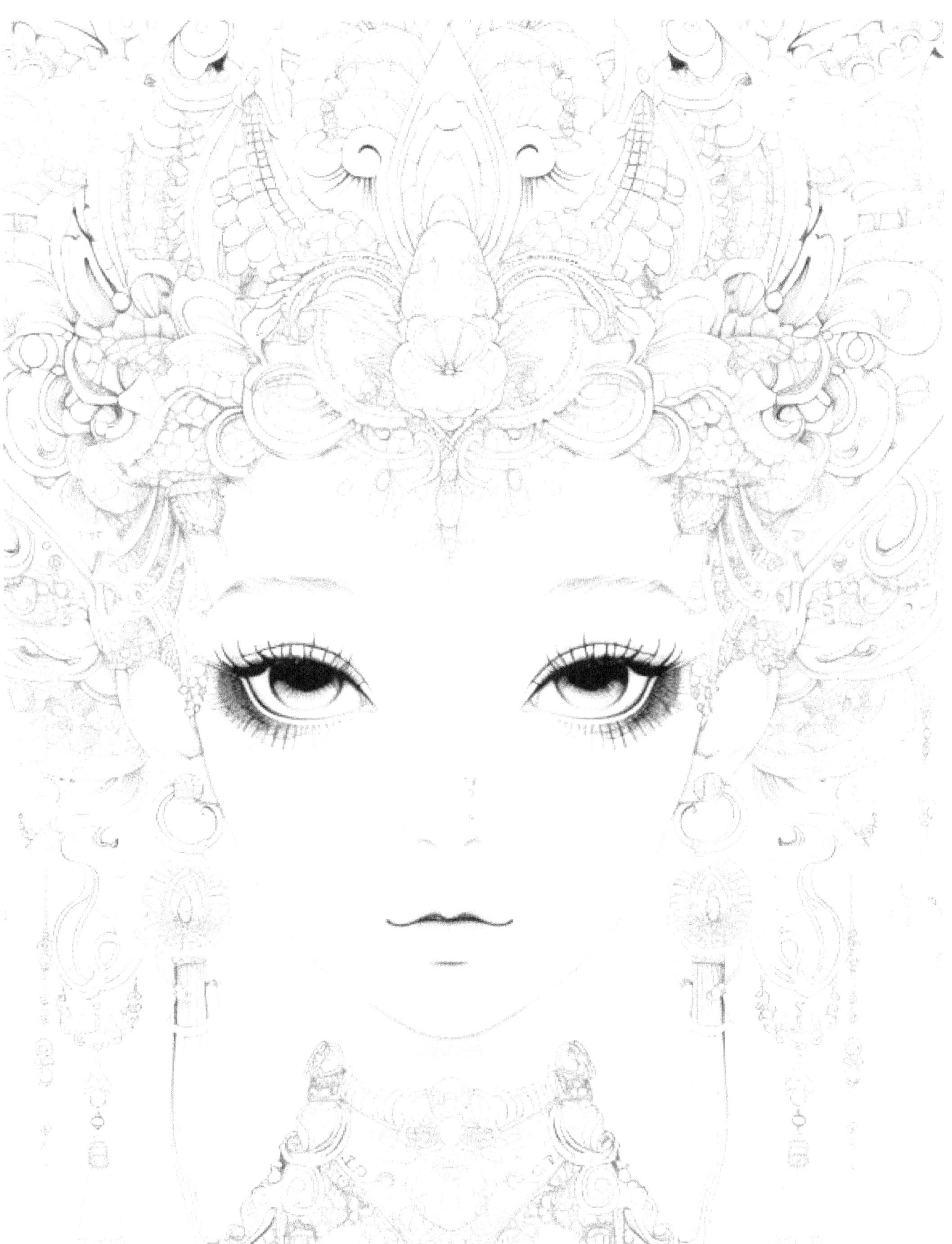

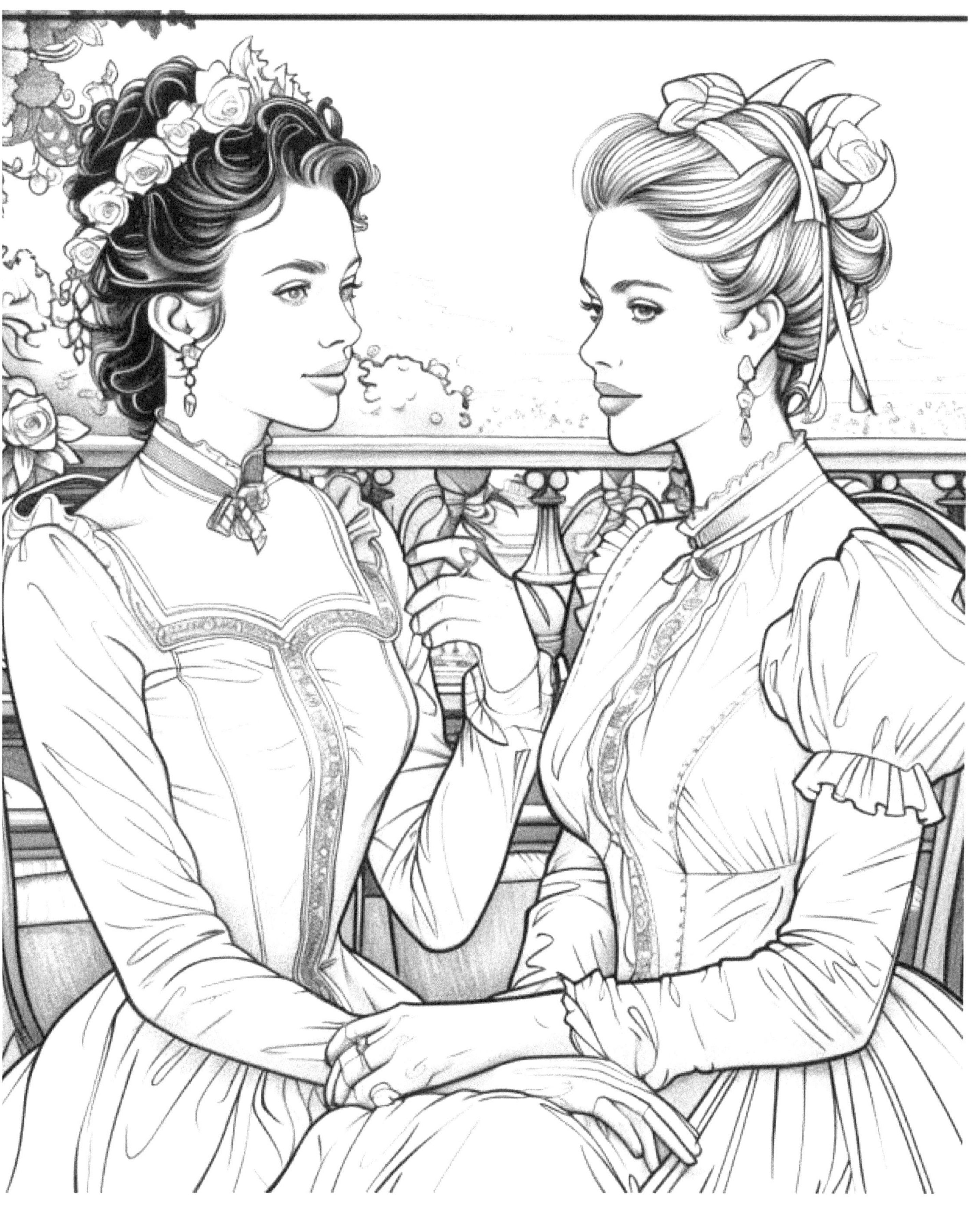

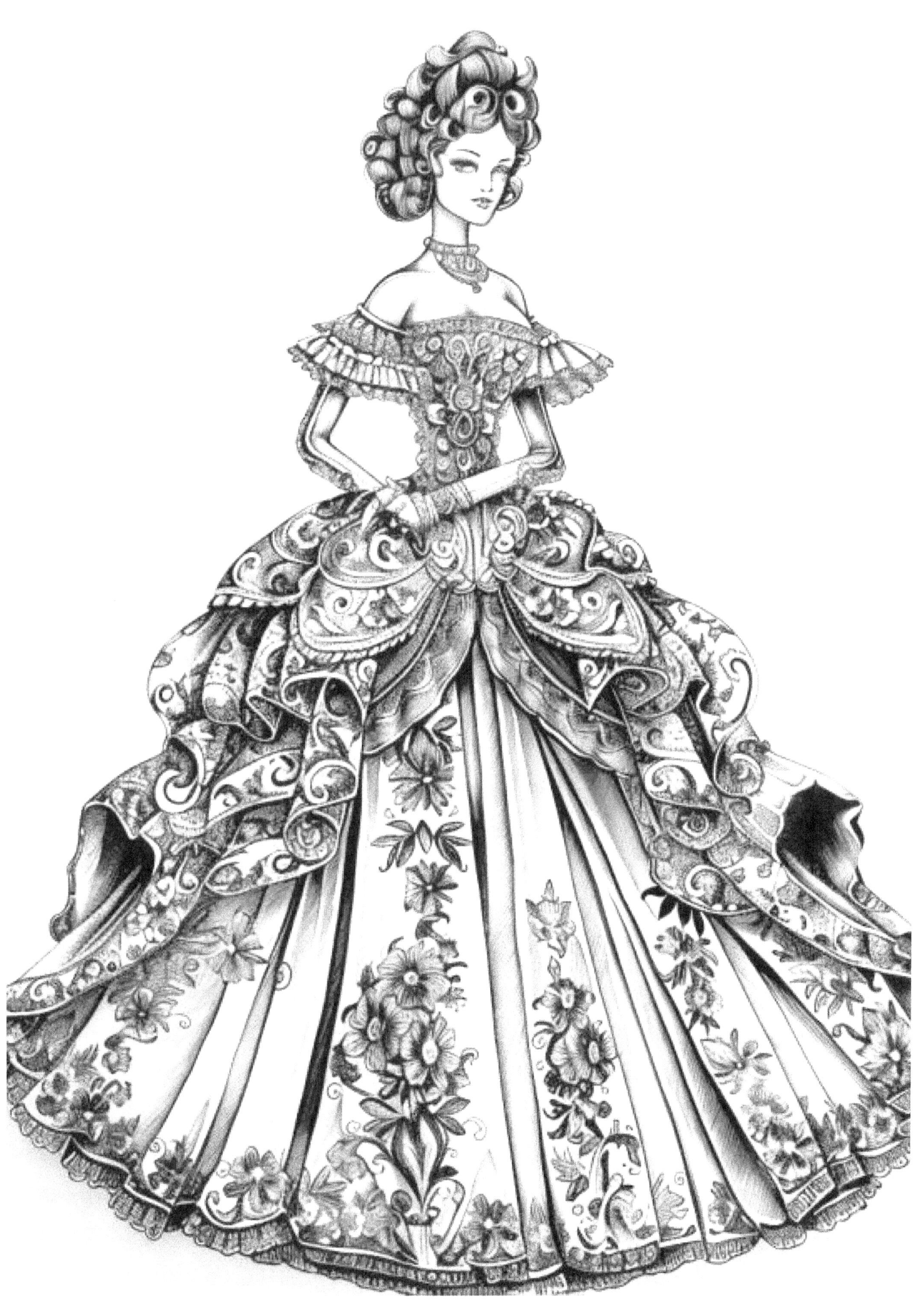

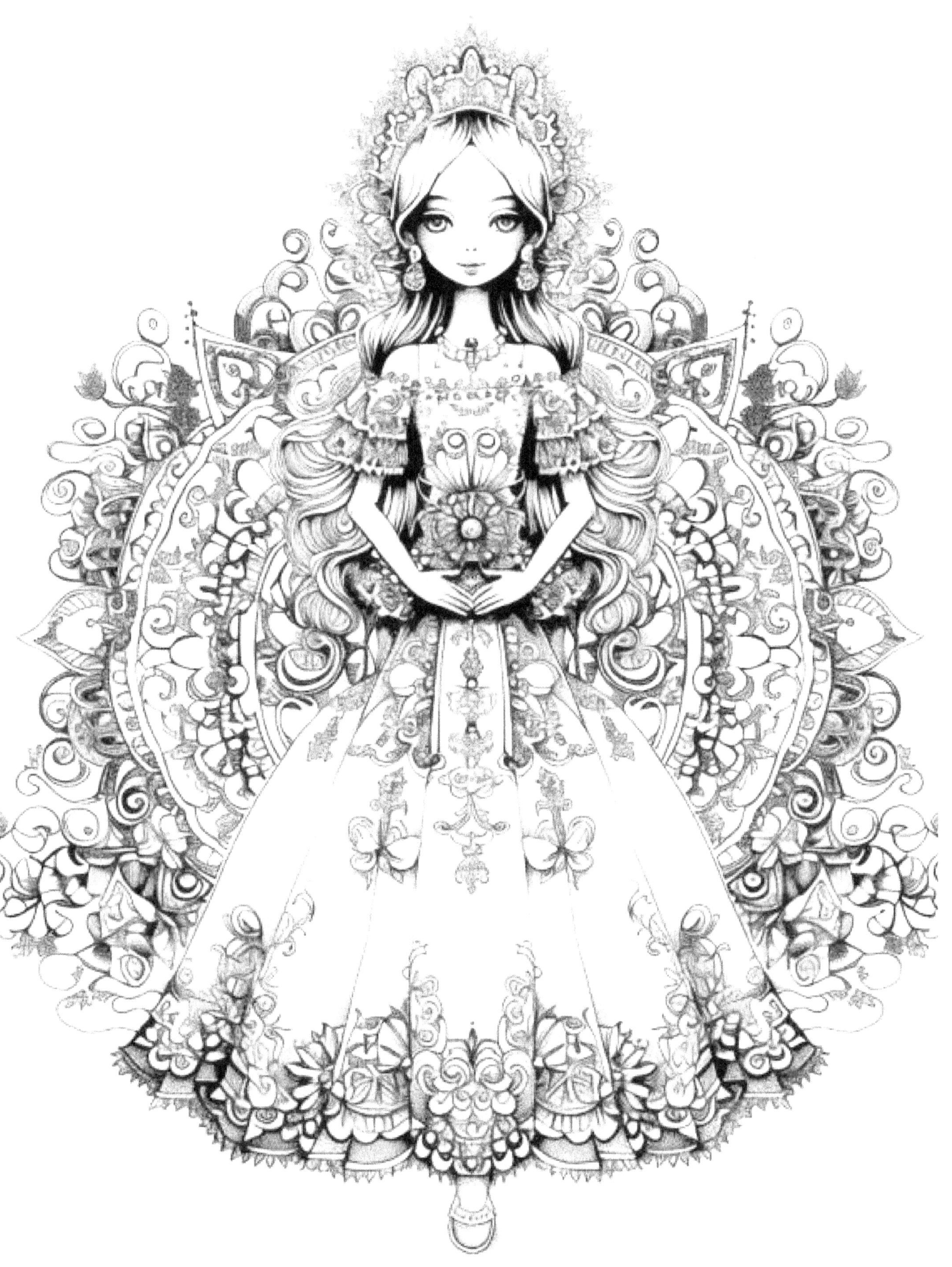

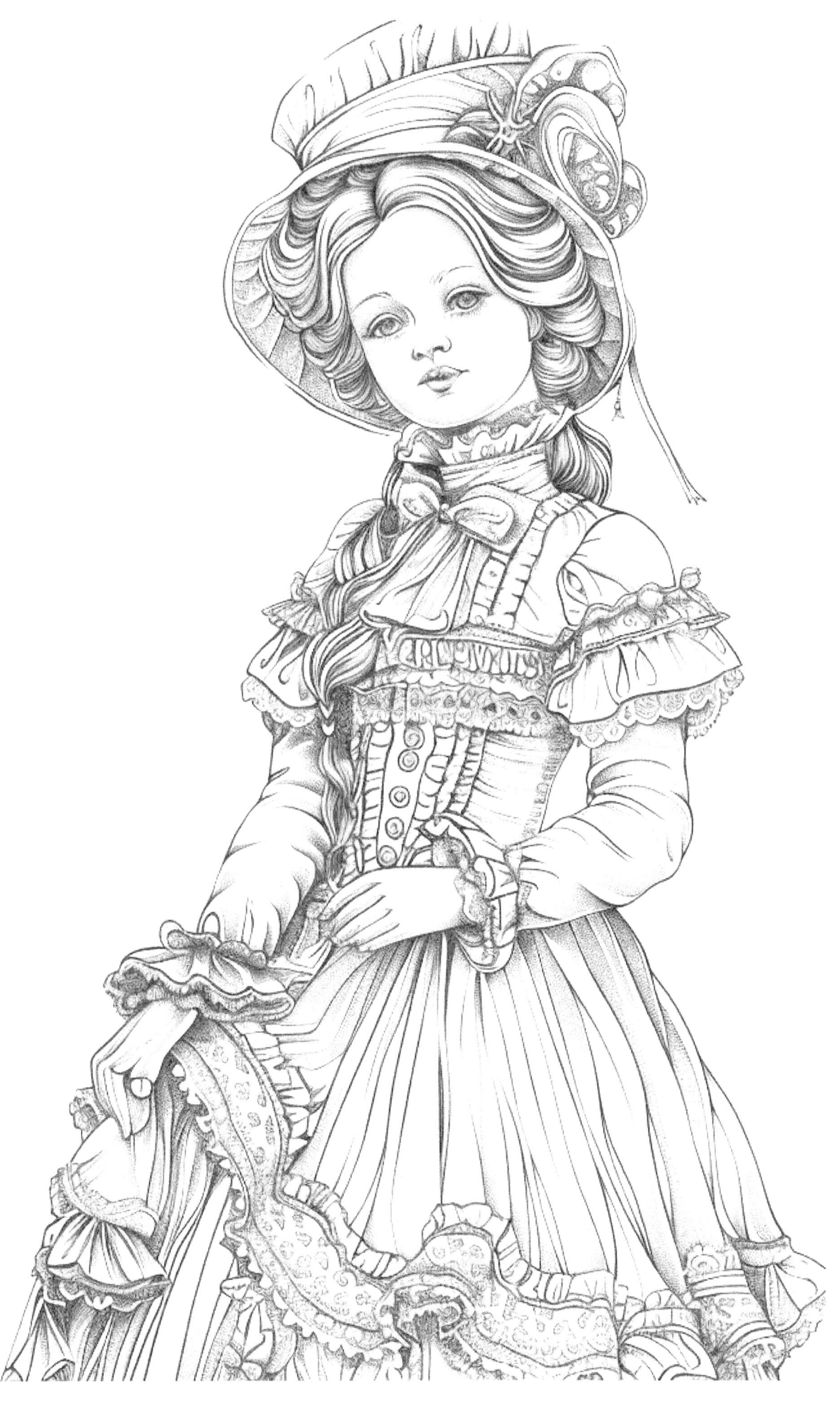

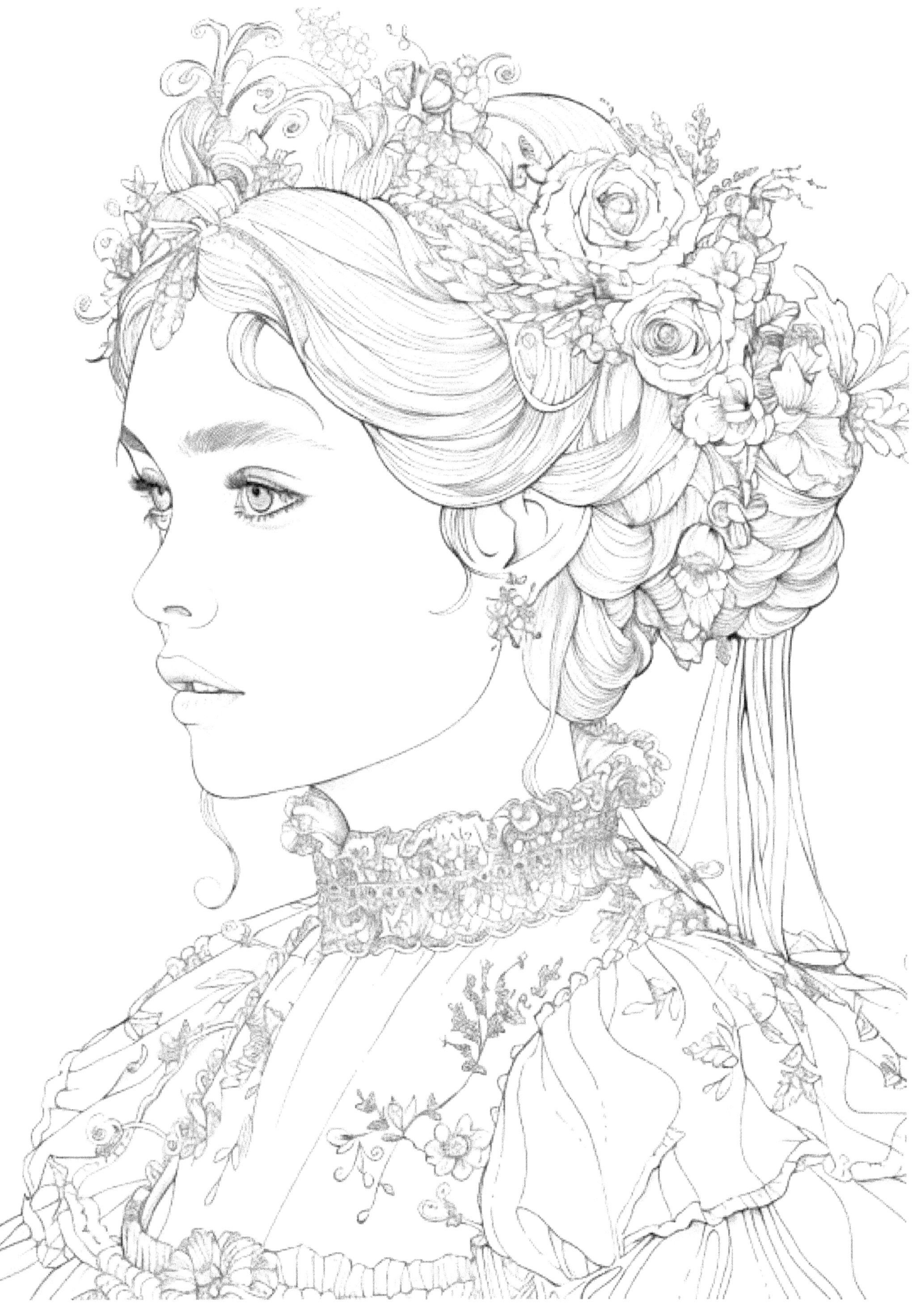

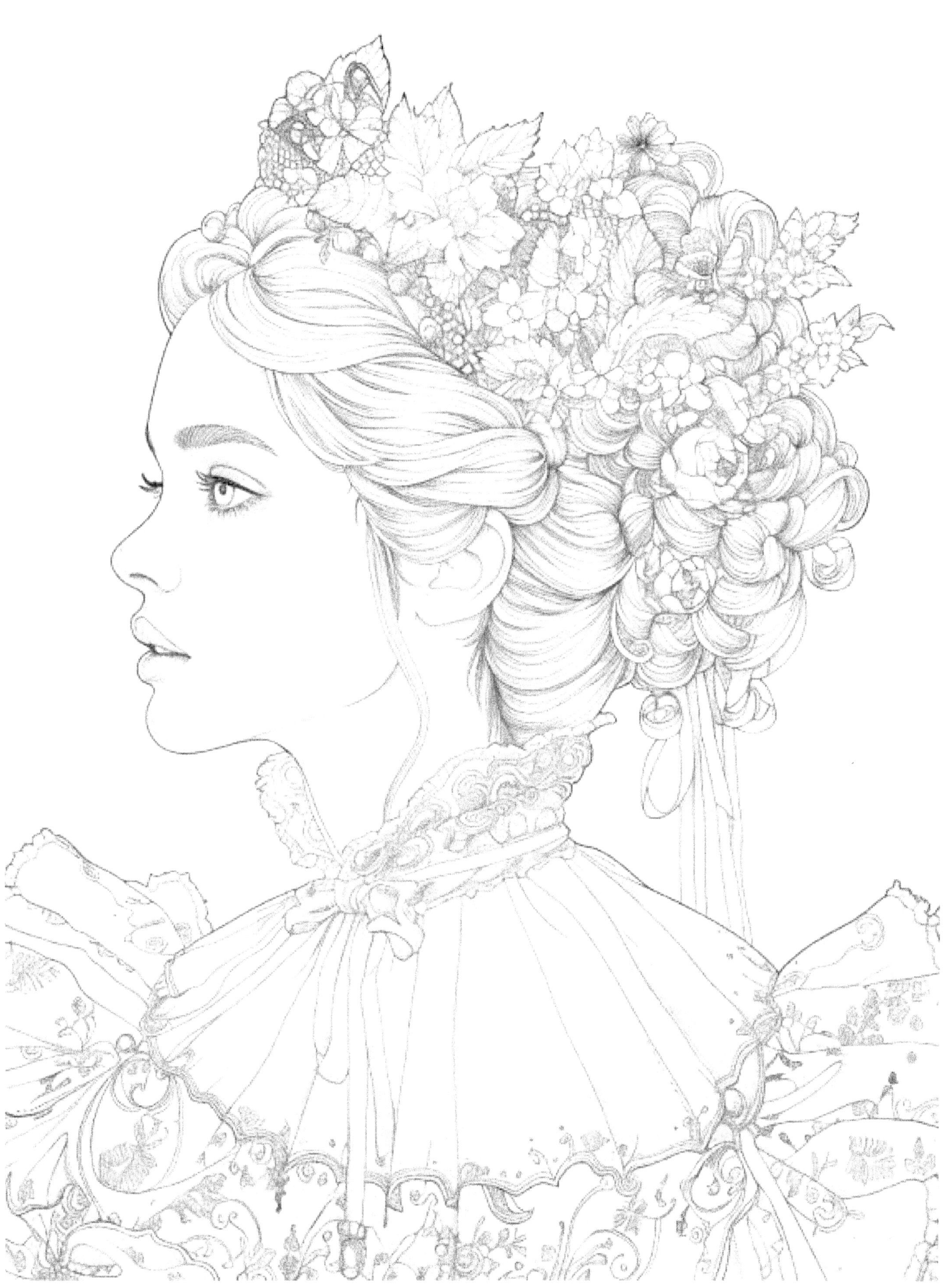

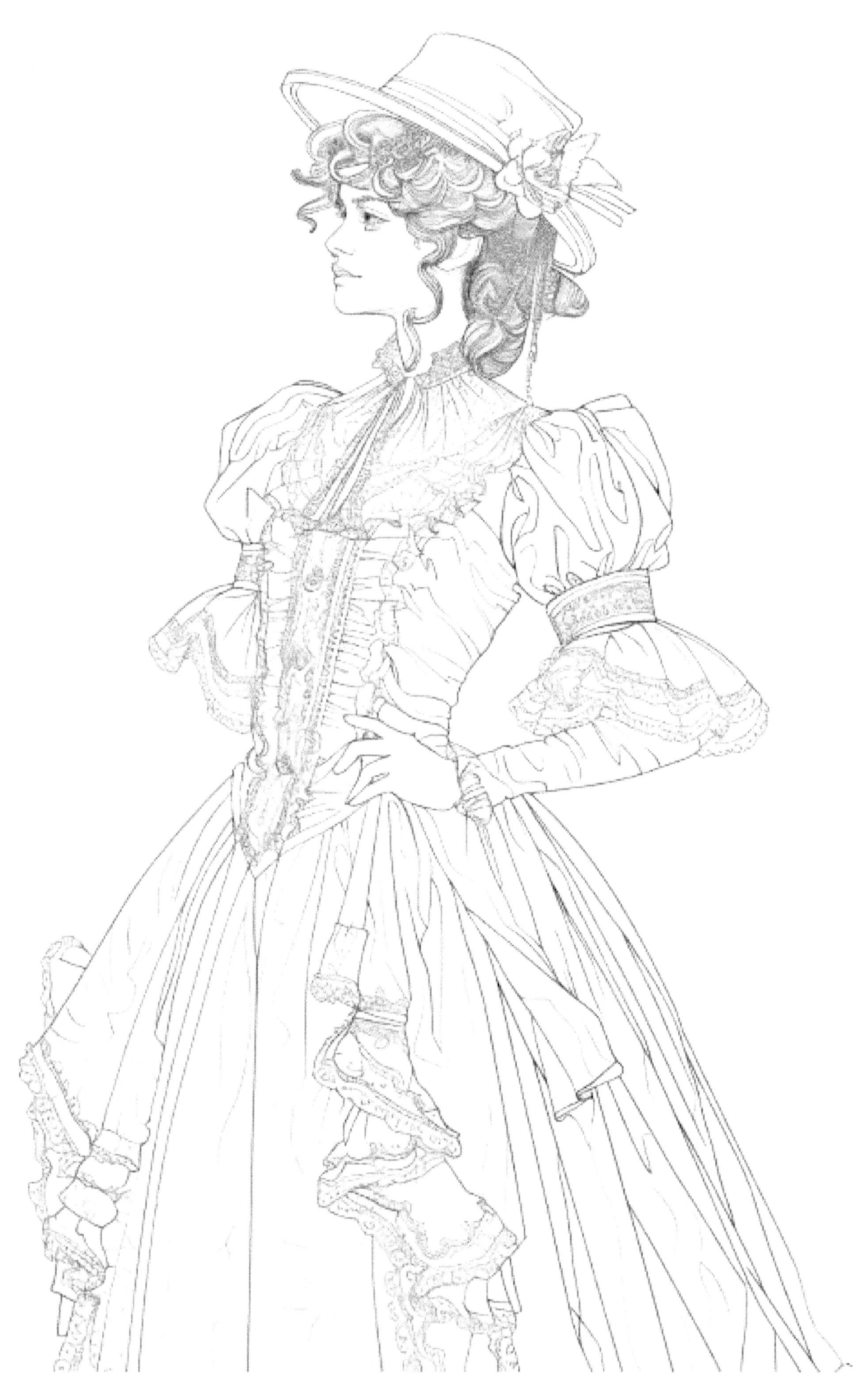

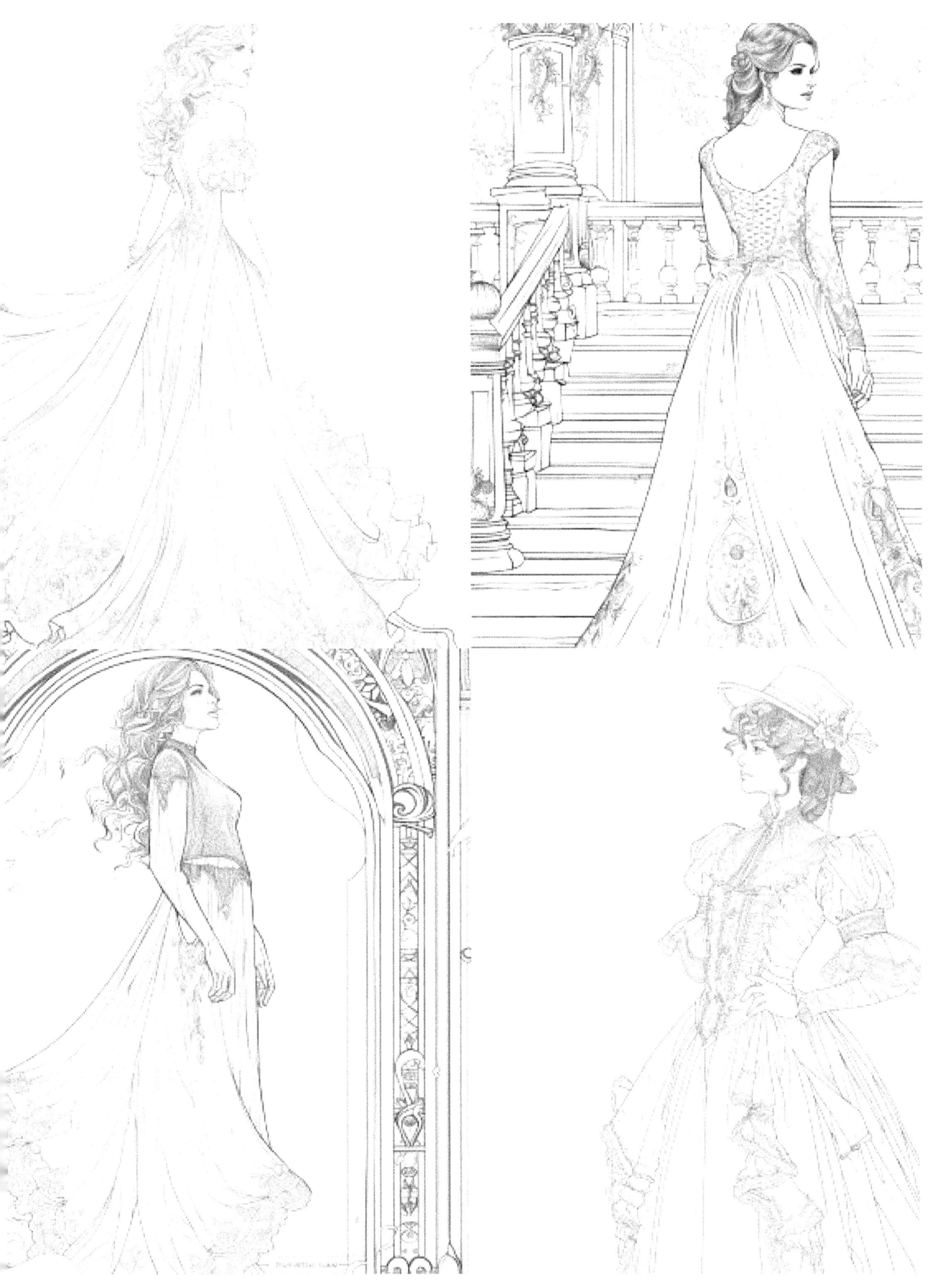

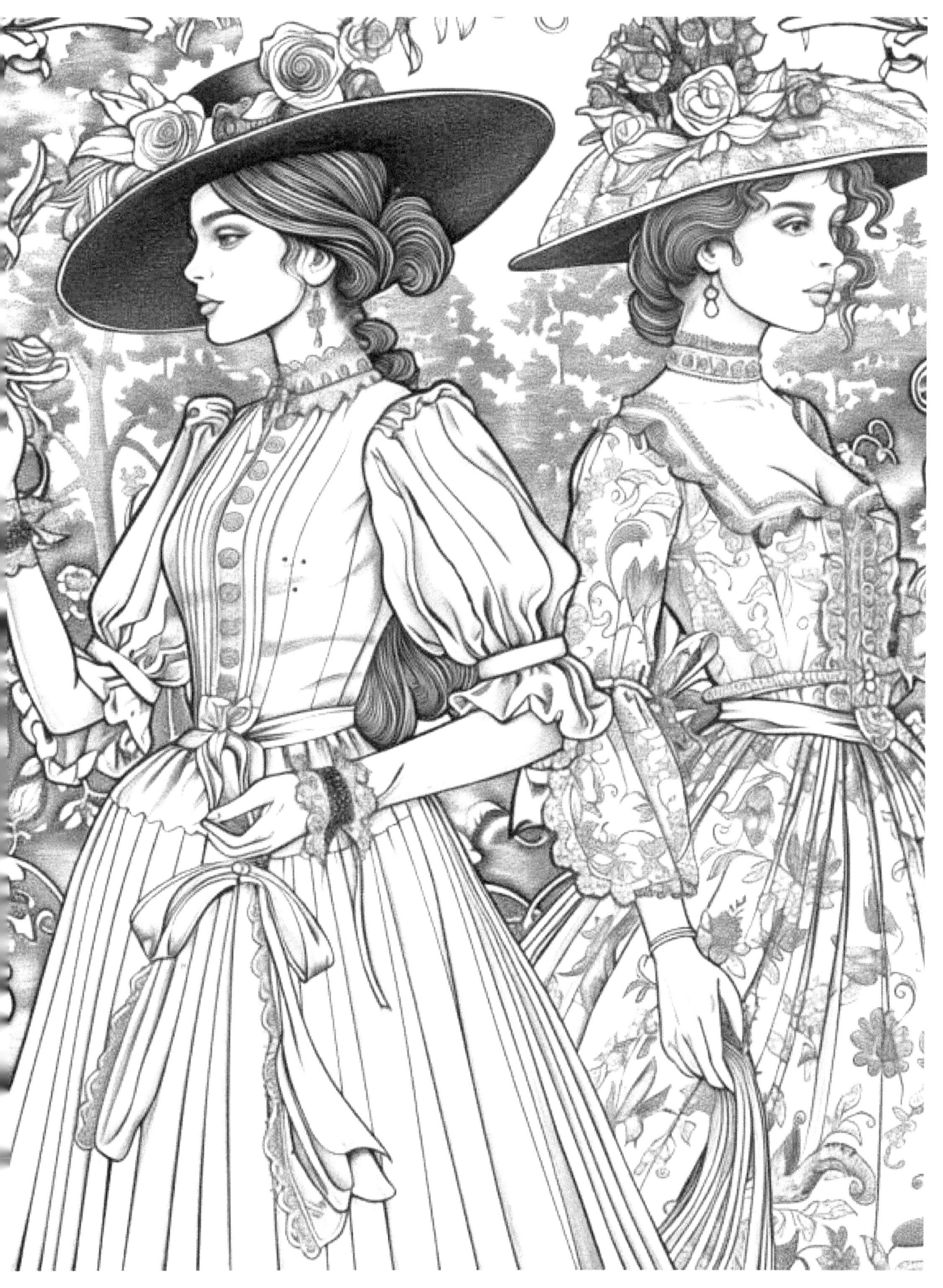

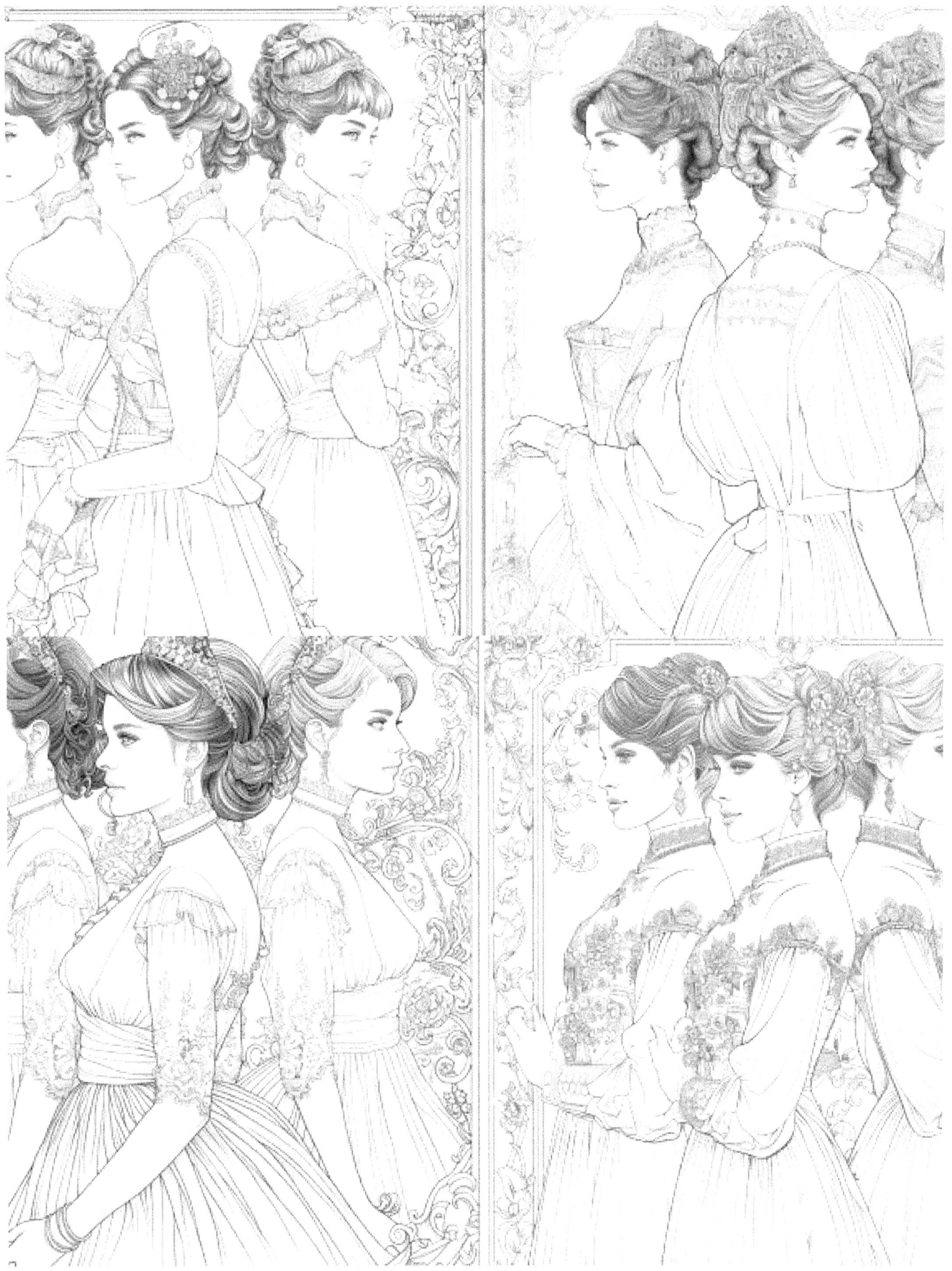

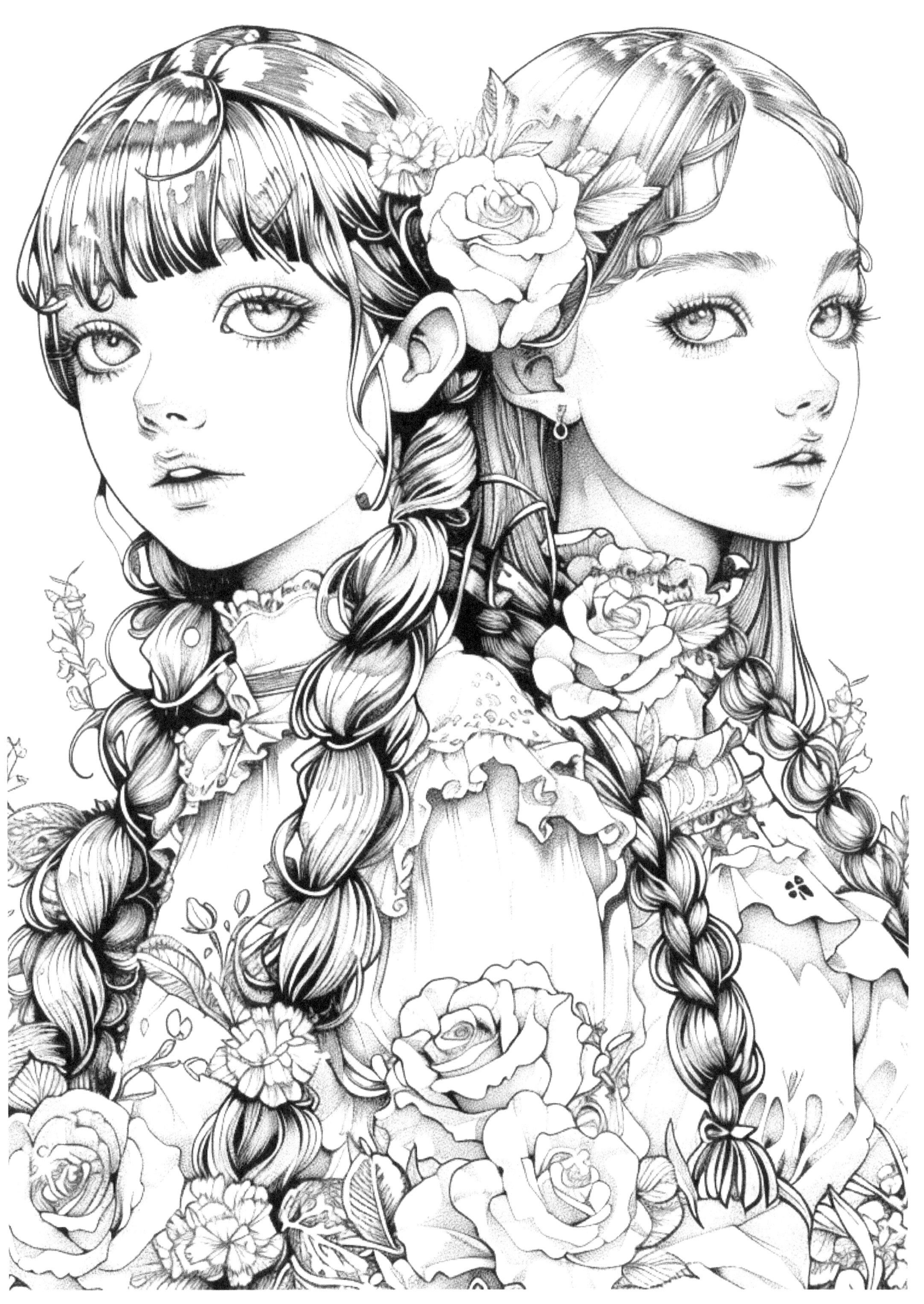

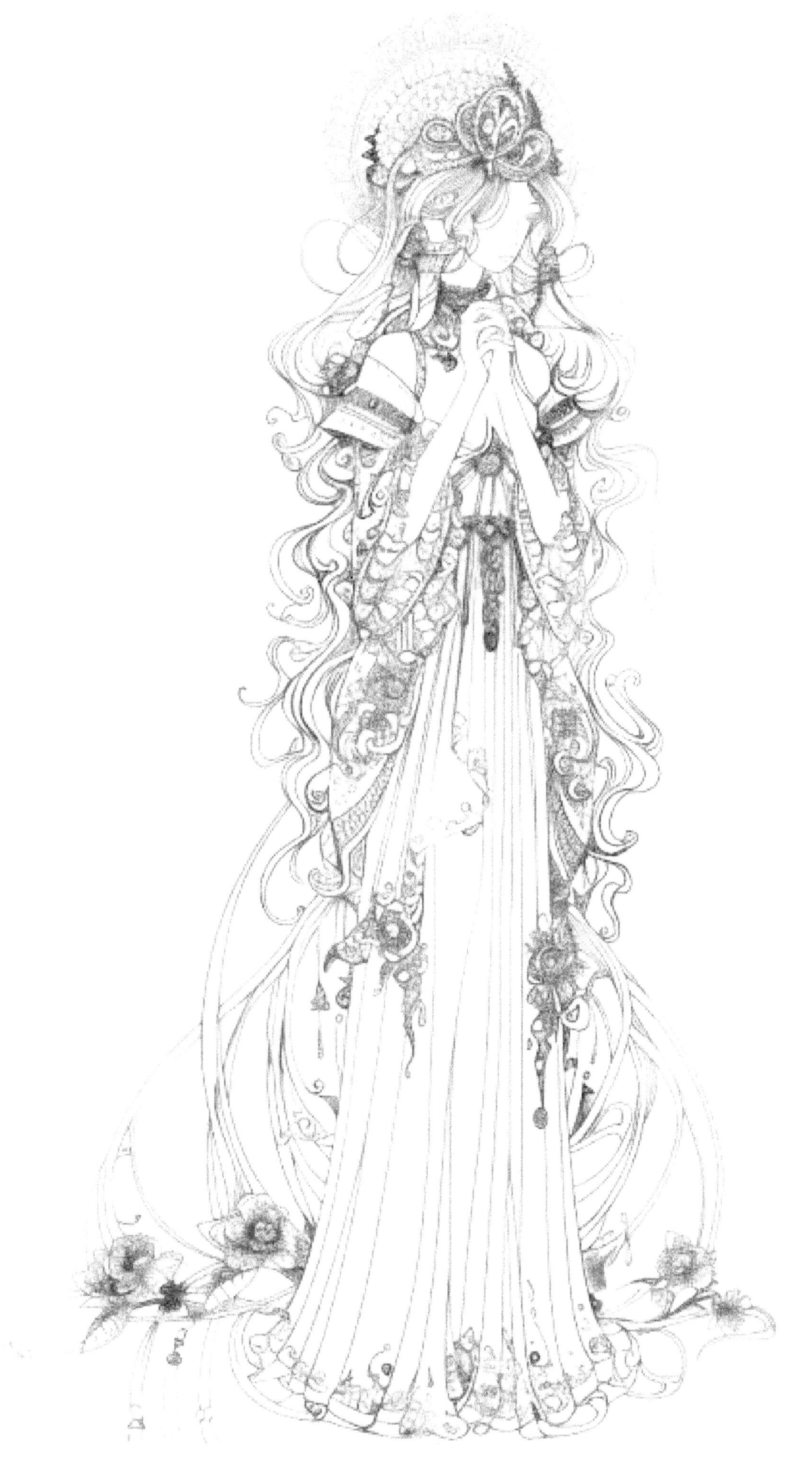